£1·99
01·25

54

FOR MARY, MARIF...
AFTER THE NECTAI

C.

C000257255

All rights reserved; no part of this book may be reproduced by any means without the publisher's permission.

ISBN: 978-1-913642-33-4

The author/s has asserted their right to be identified as the author of this Work in accordance with the Copyright, Designs and Patents Act 1988

Book designed by Aaron Kent

Edited by Aaron Kent

Broken Sleep Books (2021), Talgarreg, Wales

Contents

For those who continue;
for those who choose closure.

For Mary, Marie, Maria

Lucy Rose Cunningham

I

Mary, at 4 today

I carried more than the weight of my backpack
and the lady told me it was okay
but not what she expected,

not what I expected
as I ate breakfast ate miles
ate the last slot from
the same day appointments,

not what I expected
when the room ate my air ate my words
when the test ate my sensibility
the lady ate my stomach with
her bare hands and pressed

at 4 today

the holding clinging craving

intimacy taking place
inside,
the trouble
between us,

the individual silence of each finger padding
deriding the end of this
tender excess,

at 4 today.

***

Please hold.

***

Nectar envelops

the situation

        is getting warmer sweeter

                heavier,

she found it
there, wrapped in jelly scented curtains
pale yellow ceiling to floor,
pale yellow potpourri, warm scented

nectar is a sticky cradle,
rocking 8 weeks of lethargic lullaby
lulling longing looping back
to a night of presence,

           now

        sticky warmth
        draining to

              absence, stuck.

***

Please hold.

***

She liked its fragrance.

The gods liked sweetness
to keep their souls
tender,

sweetness saw
Aphrodite cleanse in nectar
Aphrodite put nectar in your words,
put nectar in my

womb,
her wild warmth held
tight, we clung
tight I cling
to my weight,
now clawed
shedding paper stack
tissue giving way to

red
mouths open
red pulsing to brown to

black
     is night in bedded frenzy,
        the Thames in hushed dusk,
        the emptiness when she stares at

the ceiling
4 hours into the new day,
4 tablets lining her gums,
4 hours of clotting red

sweetness,
saw Aphrodite cleanse in nectar,
put nectar in his words,
nectar in her womb.

***

Hold.

***

Basin cloud.

Ribbon clouds lace deep pink
over cranes outside,
floating in the upper part of the window,
small enough to hold in my palm.

Ribbon clouds lace deep pink in the basin,
bleeding sighs whispering across the tiles.

***

Imbibing,

drops slip between legs
the way peaches slide down throat;
honeyed sticking a reminder of aroused clinging,
in the neck of a duvet swallowing
two bodies' touch.

***

I tried calling, so I wrote instead.

***

{ For Ingeborg Bachmann }
Smoking blue

ignited slowly,

her bedcover,
the haze of
sleeplessness,

lit as she sensed blue warming to red to
white, the colour of

cotton fields to bed in   - growing tall

the flame when she caught
- seeing him leave

her hospital ceilings
from a moving trolley
- to grow or give in

to smoking ceilings inhaling bodies exhaling
cotton, to throw over her as she lay,

blue.

***

M-
she's learning to unlove
the deep blue took to be one's own.

***

11

She calls my nails
moon-disks

and I am gripping the edge of a moon,
to a vastness, to the edge of
a basin filled with stars and hot water

running in a bathroom of nails,
clipping fracturing moon-disks

ache with a shine
as the tiles in steamed chambers

where stains worsen and disks risk splintering from too
much play,
scratched reflections of
a moon no longer guiding.

***

Overcoming in the bell foundry,

soprano and alto
search each other longingly

end note, lament, *exhale.*

***

*Marie, in your house I've grown
peachy vowels;
thick, pitted,
raw.*

***

She's shaking your verses,

cutting syllables strung
around fingers legs hips
holding sounds
humming,
you speak sing silk

                                        is unravelling,

now she speaks sings
the living hum of silence,
because silence isn't absolute absence
because silence is the barm the rise
the giving way to the living skin of air.

She's shaking your verses
because silence isn't giving in,
it's the tongue taking back what belongs
it's the blade of a knife

                        sharp, it's the moment when he sees
                her silence are the words he hasn't said
                                the hands he hasn't held
                        the hurt he hasn't breathed through
                                        shaking verses.

                        ***

                        So I wrote.

                        ***

Yesterday I walked again
in the red space, in thought of you.
Yesterday you rang in the new month
and I remembered,
why I chose not to

cut the body from the pyre,
left the camphor on my tongue;
I burn so to write.

***

Maria Goretti in her loss told Me, Marie, Mother,
for to give,

forgive.

II

There grew burnished bowls and cups

of simmered tea leaves and wicks,
candles drunk with butter
wax waning, as she waited

watching, outside's indigo night
breathing into a quiet concerto,
humming, notes moving over notes,

the music becoming,
the song blushing,
admitting, after you called.

***

Summer sees

a line, letter,
mute nocturne;
black the bitter shadow of the etching.

Indigo drawn between thighs
encircling, your words.

***

Butter-spoon encased at Whitechapel Gallery.

This rounded tool cradles;
clay that lay sleeping 'til woken.

***

She told you finally of the weight, the water, the weeks of wandering,
and in tears you held her.

Her voice, grown, exhaled forgiveness;
the intensity of Vincent's screaming nights
holding her up,
the weight water wandering, away.

***

Some flowers do not take to the water. Wilting - removal.
Pressed in back covers of books
yet to be read, their colours
drained, fragile reminders.
Found weeks later, all the more beautiful.

***

And in tears you held and and, in tears-
my ampersand.

***

Bowls cups and wax fingers,
the bodies of saints burning heavenward

and when I light them,
tears prick at these small souls
wavering,

myself poured out, silk in darkness
melting,

for the second time,
everything is white gold,
bed frame my frame;
tonight I am white gold with saints,
swimming in waxen wilderness.

***

Stars, the silence of astounded souls;
vigil in the half-light,
where sleeplessness holds.

***

My ampersand; never ending.

***

Unfurling

Linden trees
smell of folds in skin folds in nights
struck with light, soft
bedding, Linden trees smell of

closed rooms, salted exhalations
struck with light, soft
kisses to the neck before
sleep-
hushed, Linden trees stir in London.

***

The room honeycombs, aglow.

***

Sleeping naked sleep,
tucked up words in cotton envelopes

always tug a little,
duvet thief,

this this this is the part when you roll
over to suffocate with a gaze

[breathe]

it is Friday morning
questioning, what is love–

settling, the space
between chest and armpit,

a change in folding
manuscript creased

corners not quite matching, hungover
anxiety that you won't read what is being said

in smudged pen/eyeliner/condensation
on windows opening to

rush-hour – slowness caressing
a room, as a city sprints on.

***

Light walks
catfooted through curtains,
like ribbon clouds, only softer.

***

My ampersand; never ending.
Never ending, we were wrapped up again, too tight.

III

Nominal voice   my dermis is all that remains

breathes, sighing   unchanged,

the warm stains   in my pants
                                                you are in my

exegesis of colour of thought   thinking,

                                                about soft lining
                                                 soft gum lining
                                                  in my mouth
                                                you are in my

excavation of thought of throat,   throat
                                                   you line
                                                my soft lining

lower tongue open mouth lips   I lower, my tongue
to long for,   and you pass
an attempt to share,   through,

to give-   as I give
                                                        in,

-yourself wholly   wholeness is
                                                 an expanse,
                                                     filling
                                            a hole is a pit that
                                             you can empty into,

feeling relief, a voice exhaling   relieving

                              as I draw another tight breath,

'you are here'   in me.

***

Sorry I was late
and you didn't get your weekend.

***

Only the godless can
preoccupy hymns house heart-

-break.

***

Sorry I was late.

***

And it's a mouth full of concrete
shoveling cement
in, to push out is
heavy, grey mixing
round and round and it goes round,
it goes

mouths full of concrete are hard
to conceive if you have a clean spade,
but tarnished spoons and pronged forks are all that's free
and I'm listening to Lana

on repeat
man, boy, ache passing through
in this building site,
breeze-blocks are lighter than
me, heavy with grey
mixing round and round and
it goes round,
the feeling that you're part of the clay
holding down house history him and her
mouth full of concrete,

is a dull stone scraping when the door goes
and your duvet is heavier than
breeze-block clay.

***

Restlessness.
Chair sofa bed. Inertia,

it goes round,
and we move with it, forwards.
Brushing hands as we walk to the station where I leave.
Leaving
no epilogue. Awareness of tender thumbs hurting,
now holding our own digits,
a delayed echo of
the loud, the night, before. Inertia.

We move, I forward to the exiting train.
Passing, chair sofa bed. We move,
mouth full of concrete.

IV

Spoon theory.

I'm running out of spoons.
Spent,
on days like these I feel white-grey
white-grey like spoons like walls on the
rounded tube,
I am staying, blending, below ground
inside rounded tunnels rounded spoons
spent running,
on days like these.

***

Regenfenster*
drops fall outside the exhibition.
Inside here too.

*rain window, at Tate Modern

***

My mother asked why;
we all have our reasons.

***

She's taking off her strong suit,
business bitch suit, I-think-I-love-you suit.
Putting them away to air.

For quite some time.

***

'There must be a reason.'
'I know,' she meant.

***

Talk to me.
Words knitted into her chest,
an amulet in her body.

***

I know.

V

to New Love

and and and oh
there's a whispering to page haze shingle salt

here -

it's a bite a fracture
a gaping in scores in bars
fingers waltzing up and down, down,
they down-fall-
-trip a little,
over themselves,
they, like her, are a tangling
subservient to blues
cobalt indigo black bottled up
in a record player,

to play
to rumble
escape, rush, rush— *run;*
it's like running, a harbouring hurtling hurting
hur— hurtle hu hu h'*hushhh*—

how to describe
you
are jazz
to lose oneself in
to lose to
Love,
        is a scattering percolating steaming,
when you're in a café
warmed by the breath of walkers,
caffeine pouring
condensation vast,

spreading,
the room is cooling
outside, distance –

a man beside me is discussing loss,
the fall, collapse,
love is collapse is sinking into jazz is taking you
taking another;
it's trembling,
the first time you met
and your heart sighs

here. It's evening,
a flight in the dark
an amulet beckoning
calling to caverns to trenches to ruin,
to dips moulding against
another,
arousal
is a juddering writhing saxophone symphony
pedaling towards
him, her, your figure illuminated

   and and and oh I want to bury myself between you and the
                                  night

in cardinal red, burnt umber,
burning thirsting need knees
drop to
a pulling,
a pulling, a pull in into onto
on grazing floorboards shuddering pulsing
gaps in the paneling;
oh Love, it's a house feeling its own weight
looking out to the eve,
it's meeting nighttime's eyes
inked with a cool white moon

calling – to the women
to the lovers the living

raging tide,
cardinal red,
burning thirsting pulsing
surge,
ruining
riotous,

                                   you held her notes
                         holding time holding gaze towards

her iteration   f f f
feeling soprano
        alto mezzo forte mezzo forte piano oh   oh to
                                a quiet bass,
holding giving way to
rushes, the sound
when bamboo stems lick each other,
breathe the words I do not yet have,
holding giving way
to a crackle to cries to swimming in nighttime,
swimming round round round and back
back space backwards is John Cage's forward thinking
thinking in silence
only slow motioning
motioning to what isn't being said
motioning to Love
is Merce Cunningham's movements,
the dips the turns the turn on to see you dance
is
oh it's a blue-rinsed litany of detritus
a long night unfurling, dreamless sleep,
it's a cradle bobbing
a river taking your body the jazz taking your mind the dance
taking your soul
Love – the verse rumble and rushing
to another,
oh oh oh and it's *here, calling–*

– Held tight. *Hold tight.*
A lift of bones and breath.

Last night I heard of his passing and I wondered could there really be
black walls of water
black walls of water of weighted nothingness clung bore broke,

                                                        breaking,

painting a river's exoskeleton,
a blue amulet's armour

arm her; this woman is breaking
slowly fracturing,
fissures mapping themselves
as the painter maps moments
he held bound tightly
knotted;
her stomach is a knot when she thinks of lost lovers,
the passing of people place time
keeps unravelling,
cold to the touch,
your hands, in the early hours;

when he takes your arms and caresses
a whispering curling conversation
that strips him her bare,
fragments freeing themselves from containment;
she's shaking a little

shaking shifting,
she thinks what it is to age –
skies losing light
a haze as alphabets confer
lettering she can't decipher,
bearing crosses
bearing the weight

of loving someone who may not love back
I you we, two boys together clinging;

Hockney takes me through
these gallery paths,
his hand reassuring as it reaches
to be held;
when he dances I think of stray drips stray fingers toes tips,
when David when he when she unravels
I become a whispering conversation,
cold touched exoskeleton
armour fracturing beams kaleidoscopic

when he dances,
painter and strokes recede, only a burst of colour remaining
and Burroughs tells me
how to catch a rhythm catch a fish,
each scale bejewelled crimson to indigo
night,

the warmth of dark skies
holding cloaked arms round our bodies like black walls of
water,
until the sun the passing the conversation shakes a little,
as light returns and visions are bared, shook free;
shook shaking
shingle, the river runs on

and on and on and
oh, there's a whispering,

                              it's this aching thought,
                 the impress of Love of ache of thought
                                    in my bedclothes,
                                  this aching thought
                              as you handle yourself
                             so gently as night fades,

grey gossamer to black,
my inked lettering
and your wild straying hair.

**

Mary Marie Maria;
Ave.

**

Heraldic dyad of white and blue,
this body a fresco against it;
the low hum of stretched out time, of stretched out limbs,
this breath voice heartbeat, a solstice prayer.

Acknowledgements

For all mothers.
Mothering comes in many forms: invaluable guidance,
infectious humour and genuine care.

Thank you, to Mum and Dad for being there through gritty
times with strength and love. To Dylan, for inspiring me
with your curious mind and quiet confidence. To Ellie, for
getting the last train from Manchester to hold me close.

Thank you to Aaron of Broken Sleep Books for giving my
writing a voice through such an innovative platform. Thank
you to Luka for reading this in the early hours and seeing its
potential; for intimacy and support.

To the nurses at Marie Stopes, for your calm and assuring
philosophies. Without you I wouldn't have grown to know
what this body really deserves – or got the implant.

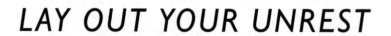

LAY OUT YOUR UNREST